LONG ISLAND
A Scenic Discovery

Photography by Steve Dunwell
Introduction by John Cunningham

Published by Foremost Publishers, Inc.
An Affiliate of Yankee Publishing Inc.

Cover: Dam Pond, by Truman Beach, East Marion   *Overleaf:* December sunset, Jones Beach

Edited by James B. Patrick
Designed by Donald G. Paulhus
Printed in Japan
ISBN 0-89909-083-4
Published by Foremost Publishers, Inc.
An affiliate of Yankee Publishing Inc.
Dublin, New Hampshire 03444

Long Island: home from a damn fine sail.

"The splendid silent sun, with all its beams full dazzling," inflamed poet Walt Whitman's love for his Long Island, then a place of simplicity, of "lilac scent" and "feather'd guests" nesting in the sand dunes.

Now, under the same sun, feathered guests might have difficulty nesting on the western half of this island, but eastward, where the beaches lie long and white toward Montauk Point, lies a land that even 19th century poets would cherish.

Nature is dominant. Great storms swirling up from the Caribbean often make their last savage stabs here before moving onto the mainland. Relentless, methodical Atlantic Ocean waves constantly rearrange the beaches. But the sky turns blue in summer, the splendid silent sun rules, Long Island lives.

Millions of people put this island to their own uses, but few ever know it fully. This *really* is an aptly named place — the largest offshore island in the United States, 120 miles from the East River to Montauk Point, 250 miles around by way of the myriad of border coves and bays.

This is an island larger than the State of Rhode Island. It encompasses great diversity and requires careful understanding.

Consider the sea coast, facing almost south rather than east like most Atlantic shores. This is the only oceanfront in New York State and it is incredible, from frenetic Coney Island to well-planned Jones Beach, from lonely beaches on Fire Island to swirling winds that tear incessantly at Montauk dunes.

From the air, the island is like a giant whale, with forks at Montauk and Fisher's Island (named not for those who go down to sea in ships but rather for a 17th century Dutch owner named Visscher). Between the forks is Gardiners Island, owned by the same family (Gardiners, naturally) for more than three centuries.

Long Island Sound intervenes between the north shore and the mainland of Connecticut and New York State. The Sound: where ocean liners ply, where yachts tack on course, where the wealthy have played for years — although sharing the bays with the baymen (Whitman was one) who see oysters and clams as their very own.

Diversity? Its very essence is the north shore.

No great surf smashes here; the relatively gentle Sound washes this strand. The great rocks and high bluffs, plus the highest hill that rises 410 feet near Huntington, are geologic-wonders, not a result of modern-day violent nature.

North shore bays are wondrous; humans could not have planned them better, but when have humans ever planned better than nature?

Gently-moving currents have reared naturally-protective walls around the bays. Inlets admit the sailors, then offer sanctuary at such as Port Jefferson Harbor (just like a bay), Stony Brook Bay, Northport Bay, Cold Spring Harbor and Oyster Bay.

Cold Spring? Visions of fresh water dance in the head, with justice, for fresh water rivers and creeks empty into Long Island Sound. The Nissequoque River is a respectable stream, especially for an island, and Lake Ronkonkoma, three miles in area, is a genuine lake.

Ronkonkoma, Nissequoque, Montauk; obviously the Indians were here first. The place names, however Anglicized, have a poetic beat of their own: *Patchogue, Happauge, Nesconset, Quoque; Cutchogue, Peconic,* even Lake Success, not more beautiful or descriptive than its Indian word, *Sacut.*

The Indians soon succumbed to beads and blandishment, first from New Amsterdam's Dutch, then from New England Puritans. The Dutch sailed around the island before 1620, established the offshore identity before settling at Breucklen (Brooklyn, their name for all the island).

Transplanted New Englanders had founded the Hamptons, Huntington, and other towns before 1640, the better to seek religious freedom and the better to pursue such secular pursuits as whaling and oyster farming.

Long Island colonists sent representatives to England to protest the tax on whale oil. When British overwhelmed Washington's army in the Battle of Long Island on August 27, 1776, they dared not venture into eastern Long Island's Yankee land.

Whalers persisted at Sag Harbor until 1871, although by 1850 the oil prosperity was dying. The "Sag" whalers built their steeple high, the earlier to see home. Many never returned. More than 30 are memorialized in Sag Harbor's cemetery; none is more than 30 years old. It is easy to imagine them in tune with the old sea chantey:

"We've come home as clean as we started out
And we didn't get a whale.
We didn't get a bar'l of oil
But we had a damn fine sail."

Home from a damn fine sail: home to Long Island. The place to live. Is *that* the island's meaning, its destiny?

People in East Hampton believe that surely John Howard Payne was thinking of their town when he wrote "Home Sweet Home." His boyhood cottage is preserved in East Hampton, where Payne lived until he set out to be an acclaimed actor and writer. He was in London in 1823, a lonely man of 31, when he wrote his much-loved song.

Home for sturdy, stubborn farmers is Suffolk County, where land is truly golden. It would be covered with homes of those who seek "open spaces" if the potato, vegetable and duck farmers succumbed to the wonders of money.

Long Island potatoes are still a household staple. As for the ducks, they won't soon disappear from menus. More than five million still quack their way over Suffolk acres; Long Island and ducklings are as intertwined as Texas and oil.

Home is Kings and Queens counties, given new life on completion of the Brooklyn Bridge in 1883 and now tied to the city by numerous umbilical bridges and tunnels. These crowded counties are Long Island, too, however much a modern Robinson Crusoe would be startled by such civilization.

Homesteaders rode the Long Island Railroad eastward. By 1930, "home" was Long Island for millions of people. Since World War II, villages have become towns, towns small cities, small cities have emerged as large cities.

Home for awhile in the early 20th century meant unbelievably lavish mansions on the North Shore bluffs, including Sagamore Hill, Teddy Roosevelt's place. Millionaires vied for a glorious place in the sun, building castles and aiming for a clear goal vocalized by one woman who patterned her home after a castle in England and boasted that *her* regal abode "was more authentic than the original."

Nearly all of the mansions are gone or tumbling down. Of those remaining, the former Phipps' estate at Old Westbury is vivid proof that for a brief time Long Island was Camelot, where the rich could emulate members of King Arthur's court.

Such matters are of no consequence to the bay people, who are happy with a proper catch of oysters. To the water people, who live on the fringes of the coves or bays, just being there is enough.

Pretension is not the way of life at most summer beaches either.

Some in July or August are crowded and noisy. Others, such as long stretches of Fire Island, do not even have roads — an anomaly in a region where the automobile rules.

Sun, sand, swirling winds; ducklings, potatoes, cauliflower; beaches, mansions, sailboats. Call them Long Island.

Aye, it's great to be back home after a damn fine sail.

John Cunningham

Bostwick Bay, Gardiners Island

Expressway and Northern State Parkway, Rosyln

Northville farm with windbreaks

Northville farm with windbreaks

North Fork pastorale, Peconic

Oak Neck, Bayville, towards Ferry Beach

Nissequogue River marsh, North Smithtown

Driveway with dogwood and azaleas, Old Field

Spring gardening, East Marion

Overleaf: Merchant Mariners race by Throgs Neck

Irrigation piping, Sound Avenue, Northville

Farm house, Manor Lane, Northville

First Place, Ladies Side Saddle, Hampton Classic

Grand Prix jumping, Hampton Classic, Bridgehampton

August evening, Ocean Beach, Fire Island

Dawn at Truman Beach, Orient Point

Uncovering seedling rows near Water Mill

Irrigation spray soaks a Southold field

Final turn before home stretch, Aqueduct

Benches and spectators, Aqueduct afternoon

Overleaf: A Saturday in July, Jones Beach

A harbor on Shelter Island

The pharmacy, Shelter Island Heights

Split rail fence, Bridgehampton

Goldenrod acres, Peconic

South facade, Old Westbury Gardens

Autumn afternoon, Old Westbury Gardens

Commuters' routine, Mineola station

Morning delivery, Ocean Beach, Fire Island

Main Street afternoon, Sag Harbor

Overleaf: Sunrise over Shelter Island and the North Fork

Fire Island lighthouse, August

Colonial home, Skunk Lane, Cutchogue

Ocean Beach haze, Fire Island

Memorial Day, Ocean Beach

Autumn haze at Lido Beach

Montauk Point lighthouse

Porch shadows, Cold Spring Harbor

Front Street daybreak, Greenport

Coast Guard station, Montauk Harbor

The flag descends, Montauk Harbor

The flag descends, Montauk Harbor

Overleaf: Preparing for Spring planting, Deerfield

Pumpkin harvest, Moriches Road, St. James

General Store steps, St. James

Tide Marsh and inlet, Lloyd Point

Rowboat moorings, Stoney Brook

The Brooklyn and Williamsburg bridges, East River

Walters Neck, South Oyster Bay

Whalers Presbyterian Church, Sag Harbor

First Presbyterian Church, 1803, Southold

Kings Point Park, Great Neck

Autumn afternoon, Kings Point

Overleaf: Dam Pond, by Truman Beach, East Marion

Barrier beach at Westhampton

Summer evening, Jones Beach

Long Island Expressway, Westbury

Amity Harbor, winter

Montauk Beach

Jones Beach

William Vanderbilt's sundial, Centerport

Vanderbilt's Eagle's Nest, Little Neck, Centerport

Lido Beach, looking west

Sand and dune grass, Jones Beach

Overleaf: Dune grasses, Lido Beach

Abandoned gas pump, Aquebogue

Wind erosion, Sunken Forest, Fire Island

Golf links, Southampton

Dinghy repair, Poquott

Duckling regiment, Westhampton

Big Duck, Flanders

Spring planting, Cutchogue

Tulips and barn siding, Mattituck

Springtime, James Lane, East Hampton

Parrish Museum, Southampton

Overleaf: Victorian veranda, Northport

Roosevelt's Sagamore Hill, Oyster Bay

Bath and dressing room, Sagamore Hill

Meadow Lane, Southampton

Marina pier, Ocean Beach, Fire Island

Hazy morning, Southampton Beach

Fog bound, Old Bethpage Village Restoration

Powell Farm, Old Bethpage Village Restoration

Christmas, South Jamesport Post Office

Poinsettias, Planting Fields Arboretum, Oyster Bay

Overleaf: Sunset off Fort Neck, South Oyster Bay

Apple blossoms time, East Marion

Equestrienne, Amagansett

North shore boulders, Horton Point

Hashamomuck Beach, Southold

Manhasset Bay, Port Washington

Oysterman, Nautical Mile, Freeport

Montauk Point lighthouse

Spring morning, Greenport

Needlework, Layton Store, Old Bethpage Village

District #6 Schoolhouse, Old Bethpage Village

Overleaf: Leffert's Tide Mill, Lloyd Harbor

Cottage Walk, Ocean Beach, Fire Island

Saturday afternoon, Brightwaters

Geraniums and marigolds, Aquebogue

"Home Sweet Home" East Hampton

Ocean Beach pier, Fire Island

Stylized sign, Jones Beach boardwalk

Dawn at Montauk Point   Polished pebbles, Montauk Point

Dawn at Montauk Point   Polished pebbles, Montauk Point

Wildflowers, Orient Point

Zinnia farm, Calverton

Overleaf: West Neck shore, Shelter Island

Lido Beach and Long Beach

Seagulls, Jones Beach

Ocean Beach, Fire Island